Baby's
First Five Years

new seasons®

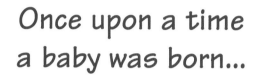

Once upon a time
a baby was born...

Here's a spot for a photo
of a brand-new baby.

Baby's name

_____

Born on

_____

Time

_____

Contents

Wonderful News!

We found out we were expecting on _____

My reaction _____

_____

_____

_____

_____

Daddy's reaction _____

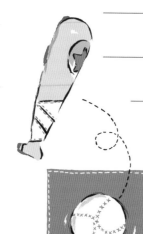

_____

_____

_____

_____

Our wishes for you _____

_____

_____

_____

_____

_____

_____

Here's a spot for a photo
of two happy parents-to-be.

Dreaming of You

We loved to think and talk about _____

_____

_____

I was a little nervous about _____

_____

_____

Daddy helped me by _____

_____

_____

The first time we heard your heartbeat _____

_____

_____

Here's a spot for
an ultrasound print.

The first time I felt you move _____

_____

_____

_____

When Daddy first felt your kicks _____

_____

_____

_____

The Perfect Name

Before you were born, we called you _____

_____

_____

We chose your name because _____

_____

_____

Your name means _____

_____

_____

Here are some other names we considered _____

_____

_____

_____

Showers of Love

We were showered with love and gifts by

_____

_____

_____

_____

Here are some memorable gifts from special people

_____

_____

_____

_____

_____

Your Arrival

Name _____

Here's a spot for
baby's first photo.

Date of birth _____ Time of birth _____

Weight _____ Length _____

Eye color _____ Hair Color _____

Place _____

When I first saw you _____

_____

_____

When Daddy first held you _____

_____

_____

What we remember most about your birth _____

_____

_____

The first thing you did was _____

_____

_____

Here's a spot for baby's sweet footprints.

15

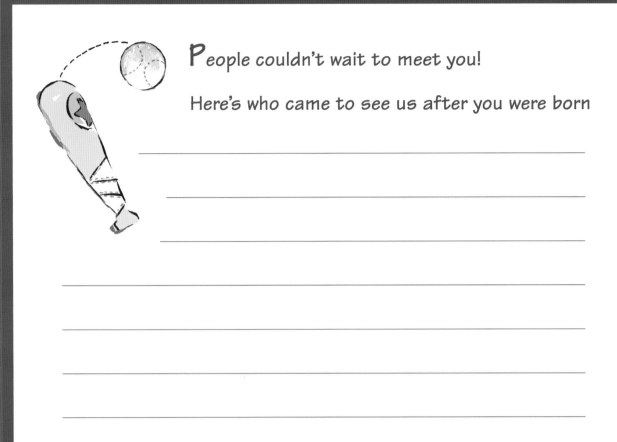

People couldn't wait to meet you!

Here's who came to see us after you were born

_____

_____

_____

_____

_____

_____

Here's a spot to save
a birth announcement.

Welcome Home, Little One

Here's a spot for a coming-home photo.

We brought you home _____

You wore _____

You were _____ old.

_____ was first to feed you.

_____ gave you your first bath.

We knew you liked it here because you _____

_____

We'll never forget _____

_____

Our Family

Great-grandparents   Great-grandparents

_____   _____

_____   _____

Great-grandparents   Great-grandparents

_____   _____

_____   _____

Maternal grandfather   Paternal grandfather

_____   _____

Maternal grandmother   Paternal grandmother

_____   _____

Mommy's family is from _____

_____

_____

Daddy's family is from _____

_____

_____

You have my _____

_____

and Daddy's _____

_____

We wonder if you'll have your grandfather's _____

_____

or your grandmother's _____

_____

We hope you've inherited _____

_____

Celebrate!

_____

_____

Place _____

Date _____

During the celebration, you _____

_____

Friends and family who joined us were _____

_____

Here's a spot for
a special photo.

Growing So Fast!

Here's a spot for a photo
of a cheerful baby.

At your first checkup, you weighed _____

and were _____ long.

At three months, you weighed _____ and

were _____ long.

You learned early to _____

_____

And you took your sweet time when it came to _____

_____

We knew you were hungry when _____

_____

We knew you were sleepy when _____

_____

We couldn't help laughing when you _____

_____

We calmed you by _____

_____

Such a face! Here's a spot for
a photo of a not-so-cheerful baby.

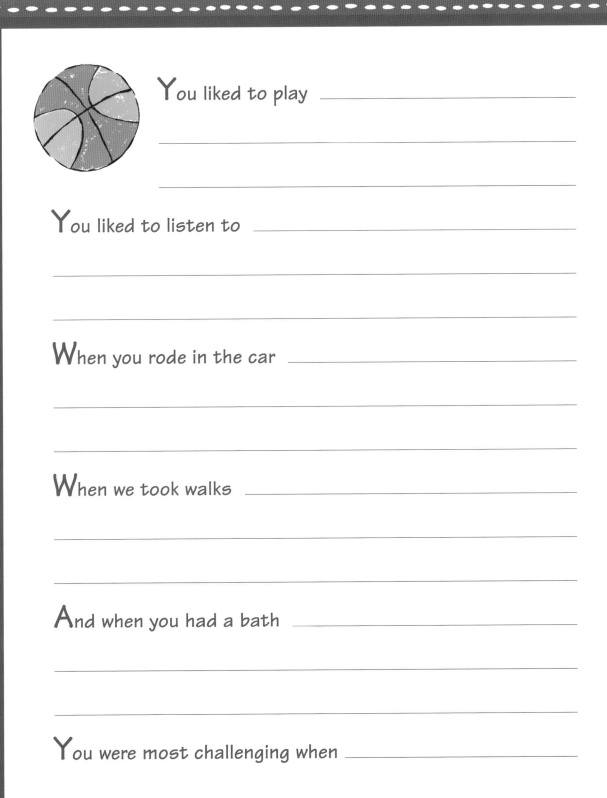

Y ou liked to play _____

_____

_____

Y ou liked to listen to _____

_____

_____

W hen you rode in the car _____

_____

_____

W hen we took walks _____

_____

_____

A nd when you had a bath _____

_____

_____

Y ou were most challenging when _____

_____

_____

Live and Learn

The best advice we received was _____

_____

_____

The worst advice was _____

_____

_____

The funniest advice was _____

_____

_____

My advice would be _____

_____

_____

_____

Happy Baby

The first time you smiled, you were _____

_____

You first laughed out loud when you were _____

_____

You laughed because _____

_____

Yay! Here's a spot for a photo
of a very happy baby.

More Firsts

Slept through the night _____

Smiled _____

Laughed _____

Rolled over _____

Said first word _____

Said "Mama" _____

Said "Dada" _____

Sat up _____

Got first tooth _____

Crawled _____

Waved hello/good-bye _____

Stood by yourself _____

Here's a spot for a
photo of a first.

Walked _____

Made mischief _____

Drew a picture _____

Sang a song _____

Wrote your name _____

Read me a story _____

A Little Story About You

_____

_____

_____

_____

_____

_____

_____

_____

_____

_____

_____

Splash!

We bathed you in the _____

_____

Bathing you was fun because _____

_____

When Daddy bathed you _____

_____

After a warm bath you _____

_____

Here's a spot for a bath time moment.

Yummmmm!

Your first solid food was _____

when you were _____ old.

Your reaction to it was _____

_____

Your favorite baby foods   You sure didn't like

_____   _____

_____   _____

_____   _____

_____   _____

_____   _____

_____   _____

Here's a spot for a photo
of a happy, messy face!

When you were a little older you liked _____

_____

_____

You always wanted to feed yourself _____

_____

_____

Baby Steps

You began to scoot and crawl when you were _____

_____

_____

You wanted to practice walking when you were _____

_____

_____

Your first solo steps were _____

_____

_____

The first time you tried to climb stairs _____

_____

_____

_____

You were off and running _____

_____

_____

_____

Here's a spot for a photo
of a toddling toddler.

Baby Talk

When you first tried to talk _____

_____

_____

You first spoke when you were _____ months old, and

your first word was _____.

When you said "Mama" for the first time _____

_____

_____

And when you said "Dada" _____

_____

_____

Settle Down

Some things you found soothing were _____

_____

Our special ways of comforting you were _____

_____

You always smiled when you saw _____

_____

Here's a spot for a photo
of a grumpy baby.

Uniquely You

Y̲ou showed your personality by_____

_____

_____

_____

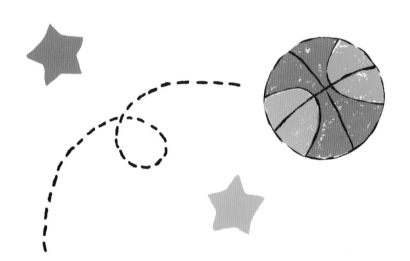

A̲s you grew, you became _____

_____

_____

_____

You were happiest when _____

_____

_____

_____

You were not pleased by _____

_____

_____

_____

Here's a spot for a photo
of a funny moment.

You had quite a knack for _____

_____

_____

_____

Your favorite pastime was _____

_____

_____

_____

We always thought you might grow up to be _____

_____

_____

_____

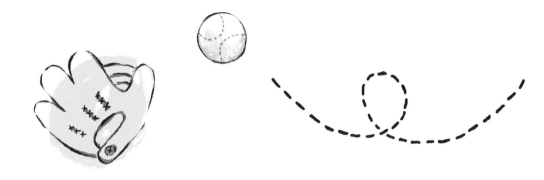

You reminded us of Daddy when _____

_____

_____

_____

You seemed a lot like me when _____

_____

_____

_____

You really took after _____

_____

_____

_____

Favorite Things

Your favorite toys were _____

_____

_____

_____

You always wanted us to read _____

_____

_____

_____

Your favorite song to sing was _____

_____

_____

_____

Some games you loved were _____

_____

_____

_____

_____

Other things you enjoyed doing were _____

_____

_____

_____

_____

Circle of Love

Your first friends were _____

_____

_____

_____

Grown-ups you loved to see were _____

_____

_____

_____

You always had a smile on your face when you saw

_____

_____

_____

_____

You called your grandparents _____

_____

_____

Some things you enjoyed doing together were _____

_____

_____

_____

Other family members you loved to see were _____

_____

_____

_____

Spring Is in the Air

The best thing about your first spring was

_____

_____

_____

When we went outside, you loved _____

_____

_____

 Here's a spot for a photo
of baby's first spring.

Summer Sun

Here's a spot for a
photo of summer fun.

Your first summer was wonderful because _____

_____

_____

_____

_____

_____

Autumn Leaves

The best thing about your first autumn was

_____

_____

_____

On your first Halloween _____

_____

_____

Spooky!
Here's a spot for a
photo of baby in costume.

Winter Wonderland

Here's a spot for a photo
of a festive baby.

Your first winter was memorable because _____

_____

_____

We celebrated the holidays by _____

_____

_____

Stylish!

Your first haircut was when you were _____ months old.

You reacted by _____

_____

_____

_____

_____

_____

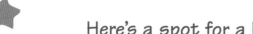

Here's a spot for a lock of baby's hair.

Here's a spot for a pre-haircut photo.

Here's a spot for a post-haircut photo.

Around the World

 Here's a spot for a
photo of a jet-set baby.

We first took a trip when you were _____ months old.

Our destination was _____

_____

_____

Your favorite thing about traveling was _____

_____

_____

Coming in First

After one year, your favorite things were

_____

_____

_____

You really grew to dislike _____

_____

_____

Some special moments from your first year with us were

_____

_____

_____

For your first birthday party, we _____

_____

_____

We were joined by _____

_____

_____

Your favorite part of the day was _____

_____

_____

Here's a spot for a photo
of the birthday baby.

From Me to You

Dear_____ ,

_____

_____

_____

_____

_____

_____

_____

_____

_____

Love,

_____

The Terrific Twos

Your favorites as a two-year-old were _____

_____

_____

_____

You didn't care for _____

_____

_____

The best moments of our second year together were _____

_____

_____

For your second birthday, we _____

_____

_____

We were joined by _____

_____

_____

_____

Your favorite part of the day was _____

_____

_____

_____

Here's a spot for a
photo of birthday fun.

Three Cheers for You!

Your favorites at three were _____

_____

_____

You really didn't like _____

_____

_____

_____

The best moments of our third year together were _____

_____

_____

_____

For your third birthday, we _____

_____

_____

We were joined by _____

_____

_____

Your favorite part of the day was _____

_____

_____

Here's a spot for a photo
of the best birthday face.

Fun Four All

Your favorites when you turned four were _____

_____

_____

You didn't care for _____

_____

_____

The best moments of our fourth year together were _____

_____

_____

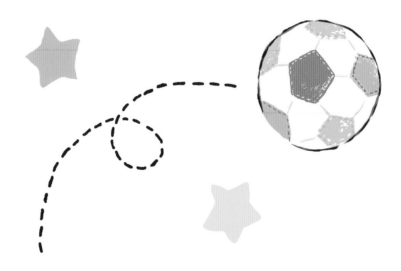

Here's a spot for a photo of
a favorite birthday moment.

For your fourth birthday, we _____

_____

_____

We were joined by _____

_____

_____

Your favorite part of the day was _____

_____

_____

High Five

Your favorites at five were _____

_____

_____

_____

You weren't fond of _____

_____

_____

_____

The best moments of our fifth year together were _____

_____

_____

_____

_____

For your fifth birthday, we _____

_____

_____

We were joined by _____

_____

_____

Your favorite part of the day was _____

_____

_____

Here's a spot for a photo
of the honored guest.

Here's a spot for a photo of your happy family.